Finding Nana

Original idea for *Finding Nana* developed and commissioned by MHA.

Partnership between MHA and the Methodist Church in Great Britain formed to be the joint publisher of *Finding Nana*.

mha.org.uk
Registered charity no. 1083995
Company limited by guarantee (no. 4043124)

methodist.org.uk
Registered charity no. 1132208

First published 2023 by MHA and the Methodist Church in Great Britain

ISBN 978 1 8585 2514 3

This is a work of fiction. Though MHA homes are real places, all the names, characters, events and incidents in the story come from the author's imagination. Any resemblance to actual persons, living or dead, or actual events is coincidental.

Production by BRF Ministries, 15 The Chambers, Vineyard, Abingdon OX14 3FE.

brf.org.uk

Printed and bound by CPI Group (UK) Ltd, Croydon CR0 4YY

Finding Nana

An MHA Special Places book

Written by Jenni Bacon

Illustrated by Sophie Parmenter

Dedications and Thanks

This book is dedicated to the memory of Ella and Len Broughton and to the people who live in MHA homes all over the country, especially those we spoke to and the amazing carers who support them. Thank you to all the people who helped bring Ellie, Jack and Nana's story to life, especially the children, parents and teachers who were our first readers and gave such helpful feedback and reviews. If you were one of them – thank you! We couldn't have made it without you.

In memory of Crispian Acher
MHA Head of Chaplaincy – South
27.5.1976–6.8.2023

"A very easy and compelling read. The main and immediate discussion we had afterwards was, will Jess's Nana go into a home, and the beauty of the book was that if she does, it hopefully won't be an unknown and frightening experience for Jess. She was quite fascinated by how the room in the care home was very much like Nana's 'real house', and that was a nice conversation as my own grandmother moved to a home after my grandfather died and she had it decorated and furnished just like her old house which I loved."

Kate, mum of Jess aged 8 years old

"Arabella and I have really related to Ellie and her family. It is really well written in a sympathetic way. The first chapter sparked a lot of questions and comments about a personal experience of having a grandparent in a care home. Arabella focused on comparing characters from the story to people she has met in real life. I got a bit upset reading the story to Arabella as it brought back fond, recent memories of my husband's grandma. I don't think this is a bad thing as it prompted discussion of our experience and memories we shared."

Emma, mum of Arabella aged 7 years old

"I have read many books about care homes for children over the years but I have to say this is the best.

"It is emotional – I could feel myself welling up reading. It is informative and written in an easily relatable style for children. I love the relationship with Ellie and her brother!

"A wonderful piece of work that has made my day."

David Moore, Dementia Lead Specialist, MHA

"The best of care and support shines through this story. Through the children, we discover that care homes enable people to contribute to their community, maintain their closest relationships, and develop new friendships. The chaplain reminds us of the spiritual aspects of care and that we are called to celebrate people's skills, gifts and inherent value. At their best, care homes are places where people come to live, love and have fun, doing the things they enjoy."

Anna Dixon MBE, Chair of the Archbishops' Commission on Reimagining Care and the author of *The Age of Ageing Better*

Contents

1

Not the way to Nana's

Ellie was looking out of the car window at the blurry trees, trying to block out her little brother's voice. Every five minutes he said the same thing.

"This not the way to Nana house."

Jack was three. He was trying to be helpful. But they'd been travelling for half an hour now and Mum had started using her extra calm voice, so Ellie knew that when Jack said it again, any minute now, Mum was going to yell.

"This not –"

"Gah!" yelled Mum. "Jack, love, please stop! Ellie," she pleaded, "help me please, will you? Read Jack a story or something? And shut that window!"

Ellie was nine years old and had seen it all before. Mum said she hated shouting but she was very good at it. Jack's little face crumpled, there was a pause, and then he started to wail. Ellie rolled her eyes. *Well done, Mum,* she thought.

They pulled up at a traffic light.

"Look, Jack" said Ellie. "Look!"

She did her 'big sister' voice. "A fire engine! See!" Distractions didn't come better than a fire engine.

But Jack was upset. "NOT the way to Nana's! Jack *know* way to Nana house. Want. Go. Nana. House!" He actually stuck his bottom lip out.

Ellie reached across the seat to him. "We're going to see Nana right now! She's just not in her house any more, Jack. She's gone into a home."

"The Care Home, Jack, remember?" said Mum, looking in her mirror at them.

Finally, Jack seemed to be listening. He looked at Ellie and sniffed. *He really is just a baby*, she thought, and smiled at him.

"What a Care Home?" he said.

Ellie looked at him. *Gone into a Home* was easy to say, but what did it really mean? Mum had explained it one night last week when Jack was in bed – that this was why they hadn't been able to see Nana for a while. That Nana was going to be fine, but after the last stay in hospital she couldn't go back home. That, actually, she wouldn't ever live in her own home again.

Ellie opened her window again. Her face felt too hot.

"It's what we were talking about this morning, Jack," said Mum over her shoulder. "A Care Home is a place where Nanas and Grandads go when they need a rest, remember? And...well...sometimes they need to stay there forever –"

"Forever?!" Jack looked outraged. "What about Nana house?"

"Nana's house is too big for her now. She can't look after it. And it's getting dangerous for her –"

"Dangerous?!"

"She keeps falling over, Jack!" Ellie said, and threw herself back in her seat.

Jack didn't understand, she could tell, but he was quiet for the rest of the journey. Perhaps he was thinking about how often he fell over, and whether he would be sent away from home if he did it too much.

❖

There was a gravelly crunch as Mum pulled into a car park outside a big yellow brick building.

"Here we are!" she said, brightly.

There were trees and bushes growing all around and Ellie thought it looked a bit like the outside of her friend Poppy's block of flats. *Did Nana live in a flat now?* Ellie wondered.

She counted 12 cars while Mum let Jack out of his seat and wondered who else lived here. Nana had been friends with all the neighbours in her old street.

"Out we get Ellie," said Mum. "We're here now."

But where's here? thought Ellie. Suddenly she didn't want to go in.

What was Nana doing here? Would she really be here forever? What about all her stuff? What about her garden?

And would Oscar be able to come and live here with her? Oscar was Nana's big ginger cat. Ellie was enjoying having him sleep on her bed, but Nana loved Oscar and Ellie knew she'd be missing him.

"Come on, love," Mum said again, and Ellie slowly climbed out.

Jack was already clutching his scooter, jumping up and down. He'd spotted the smooth red tarmac of the path outside the building.

"Look," said Mum gently, bending down a bit and rubbing the side of her head. "I'm sorry I shouted before. It's been a long couple of weeks that's all. Mum's a bit tired."

"Jack not tired!" shouted Jack, and he jumped onto his scooter. "Let's go! Zoom!"

So then Mum and Ellie were half walking, half chasing after him and Mum was calling, "Jack, wait!" and there was no time for Ellie to ask her any more questions.

2

LAIDEE

They reached the entrance – a pair of glass sliding doors like the ones in a supermarket – but Jack didn't even slow down.

"JACK!" Mum called, but he was already whizzing away for another loop of the car park. Mum groaned.

"Wait here, Ellie," she said, and jogged after him.

Ellie stood under the porch and pushed her hands deep into the pockets of her dungarees. Her tummy felt weird – a bit like when she had to speak in assembly. She wished she'd run after Jack.

She moved closer to the door to peer inside and it slid open automatically. A smell of school at lunchtime wafted out. It was so different from what Ellie was already starting to think of as Nana's 'real house'.

Nana's 'real house' was black and white with a red, sloping roof, a garden at the front and back, and a little gate that was always a bit broken. The front door was yellow with glass you could look through, and inside there was an arch into a big living room covered in light green wallpaper with tiny yellow, pink and orange flowers. Ellie had spent a whole afternoon once counting every single flower on the wall over the fireplace, but she'd never been able to count them all.

In summer, the sliding door to the back garden was always open. Nana's house smelled of the flowers she grew, and the perfume she sometimes let Ellie try on. Ellie's Grandad had died just before she was born, but there were pictures of him on all the walls and Ellie liked to make up stories about him that she sometimes told to Nana but never to Mum.

They didn't need to drive to Nana's, because you could get there by bus. And Ellie could walk there from her school. Ever since Ellie was Jack's age, Nana had looked after her after school until Mum got home from work. And every Saturday morning too. Nana was going to look after Jack as well when he started school, but suddenly everything changed.

Nana fell and hurt herself badly and had to spend weeks in hospital. Ellie went to Poppy's after school instead.

Now, standing here outside the Care Home, she realised she might never be in Nana's 'real house' again. No more Nana-hugs in the kitchen.

She thought again about her holiday homework.

Mrs Lewis wanted everyone to make a scrapbook or model showing the class everything about their 'special place'.

What am I going to do? thought Ellie. *I've lost my special place.*

❖

"Are you alright, my dear?" said a voice just behind her, and Ellie jumped.

A tall lady with long braided black hair, a huge scarf, big gold earrings and bright orange glasses had just come through the door. She carried a large tray of flowers, stones, beads and other oddments. A big bowlful of sea shells wobbled on top of it all.

"Sorry!" laughed the lady. "I didn't mean to make you jump." She looked around.

"Are you by yourself, ah...?" She raised her eyebrows and leaned towards Ellie in that way grown-ups do when they want to know your name but don't want to ask.

My Special Place
Eleanor Hodson

Ellie's throat felt tight but she managed to stammer out "Ellie..."

"Ah, Ellie..." said the lady with a big smile. "What a lovely name. You are here by yourself, Ellie, are you?"

Ellie shook her head and pointed towards the far side of the car park. Mum had caught up with Jack right next to their car and was trying to wrestle the scooter from him while he cackled with laughter.

"Ah-ha!" the lady laughed again loudly. "Your little brother?"

Ellie nodded.

"My son was just like him!" the lady said. "You've come to visit someone, Ellie?"

"My nana –" said Ellie, "I mean, my grandmother."

The lady beamed. "Your nana will be glad to see you, I know. And what is her first name, my dear...?"

Ellie wondered who this lady was to be asking all these questions and it must have showed on her face because the lady shook her head and said "Sorry! Who am I, isn't it?" She laughed again and put a hand underneath the swirl of her scarf to uncover a badge with a rainbow on it.

"My name is Olaide, but everybody calls me Laidee." She chuckled.

"I am the Chaplain here, so it is my job to know everybody!"

Ellie found herself smiling too.

"Well, my nana's real name is Margaret," she said, "but everyone calls her Maggie. I just call her Nana, though. She's my mum's mum. She just moved here."

"Ah, Maggie! Yes! Now I know. A lovely lady. She has been a very great help with our garden already."

"Really?" said Ellie.

"Yes! Your nana knows a *lot* about flowers, Ellie. Is this your first visit?"

"Yes", said Ellie. She wanted to ask Laidee more

about Nana and the garden but Mum and Jack had reached the door, puffing and panting.

"Hello! You must be Ellie's mum?" said Laidee, reaching out a hand.

"Yes," said Mum, shaking the hand, "my mother, Margaret Hodson, moved in a few days ago."

"I am the Chaplain here. My name is Olaide. We are so glad to have Maggie with us. I hope you feel she's settling in?"

"I *think* so," said Mum. She tilted her head and did that thing with her eyes that said she didn't want to 'say too much in front of the kids'. That was usually when Ellie started listening hardest.

"She's certainly been telling me a lot about the garden project – that sounds wonderful."

"Yes, we're very excited about it, and your mother is a gold mine of information when it comes to planting! You know, she may be in the garden this morning. Would you like me to let you in?"

"Actually, I need to speak to the manager first. It may take a while," said Mum.

"In that case, let me help – I can take Ellie and her brother for a little tour while you do that – as it's their first visit?"

"Er..." said Mum. "Jack can be a bit of a handful..."

"I have five children!" trilled Laidee. "Would *you* like to help me in the sensory garden, Jack?" she said, stretching out a hand.

"Jack go mummy!"

Laidee laughed. "Ok then! But how about you, Ellie? Would you like to help me while your mum does the paperwork? We might find your nana in the garden?"

Ellie realised she badly wanted to find Nana first, before Mum and Jack did.

She whirled around – "Can I, Mum?"

"Well, we're supposed to meet Nana in the cafe

in half an hour, so that's ok with me. But stay with Laidee though, ok?"

And then Mum and Jack were gone and Laidee and Ellie were left alone in the porch.

"Aren't we going in, too?" asked Ellie.

"Let us go around the back first to drop these off. Then I will give you a little tour. Whoops!" She nearly dropped her shells. "Can you carry these for me?"

She handed Ellie the bowl and set off, scarf billowing behind her in the wind like a sail.

3

The Sensory Garden

"What's a chaplain?" asked Ellie, as they followed the yellow brick path round the side and back of the building.

"Ah! A good question!" Laidee thought for a moment.

"Let me start with church. Have you ever been to a church, Ellie?"

Ellie had sometimes been to church with Nana. She enjoyed the singing, and sometimes she even helped with the coffee and squash. She nodded.

"Church is a place we can meet with God," said Laidee. "A chaplain's job is to take the *feeling* of church outside the *walls* of church. We go into hospitals, care homes, schools... and we try to show people God's love when they need it. Lift their spirits!"

Apart from Nana, Laidee was the first person Ellie had met who spoke that way about God – kind of as if they'd met. She remembered the way Nana would bend her head and close her eyes when she was lighting a candle for Grandad Bill.

"Do you say prayers for people?" Ellie asked.

They'd reached a tall wooden gate set into a brick archway. Laidee turned and looked at her. Behind her glasses were eyes that were a bit like Nana's, Ellie thought – clever, and smiling.

"You know, Ellie, a lot of my time is sitting and chatting with people. We do a lot of laughing here. So good for the soul!"

Ellie wondered what her teacher, Mrs Lewis, would think of a grown-up being so enthusiastic about chatting. Probably it was different if it wasn't in class, she thought. "Do you live here?" she asked.

This seemed to delight Laidee. "Well! My family would say I do, eh! Now, where *is* that key?"

Ellie decided she liked Laidee, who was still chuckling as she patted around her pockets.

With a sudden "aha!" and a big smile, Laidee reached under her enormous scarf and produced a large bunch of jangling keys on a cross-shaped key ring.

As the gate swung inward, the traffic noise faded away. It was like stepping into a secret garden, or the outdoor bit of Nana's favourite garden centre, Ellie thought. There were little trees in pots, yellow gravel paths, and flowers everywhere. The whole thing was closed in by a tall fence that had been painted in rainbow-coloured stripes.

There was an old-fashioned bike with a basket full of flowers, and benches underneath two tall blossom-covered trees.

A very old man sat with a blanket over his knees and a girl, who looked the same age as Ellie's cousin who was in college, sat next to him.

They were both laughing as she brushed the petals out of the man's hair. At the sound of the gate, the girl turned to give Laidee a wave, and Ellie could tell from her badge that she must work here.

❖

In the middle of the garden was a large paved circle with a small round table off to one side. Three round tubs were raised up on wooden legs and a man with a big bunch of keys round his neck was tipping a bag of soil into one of them.

"Hallo, Alan!" Laidee called as they came up the path towards him.

"Alright, Laidee," Alan nodded without looking up and Ellie noticed he was wearing a 'Mr Grumpy' Mr Men t-shirt.

Laidee placed her bundle down on the table and

whispered, "Alan helped to build this garden. He's not as grumpy as he pretends to be."

"What are all these things for?" Ellie asked, putting down the shells.

"A sensory table for the sensory garden! I want people to be able to touch and hold the different objects. Aren't they lovely?" answered Laidee.

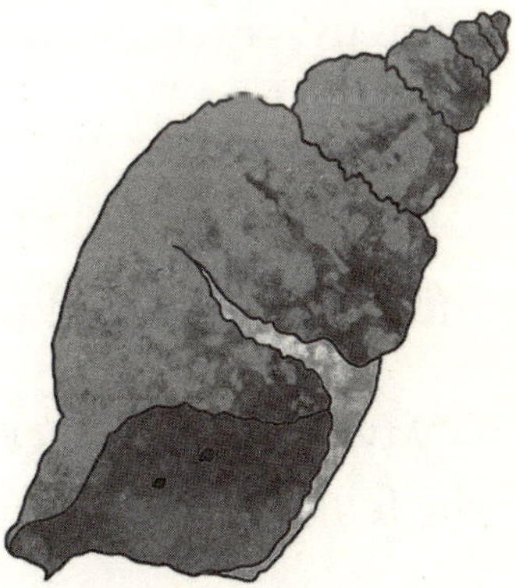

"Why?"

"Why, my dear?"

"Why touch and hold them?"

Laidee paused to think. "Hmm, how to explain... have you ever been to the beach, Ellie? Perhaps picked up a shell?"

Ellie nodded.

"Well, holding one of these shells might take you back to your memories of days at the beach. And that might make you happy, don't you think?"

Ellie picked up a shell and turned it over in her hands.

"My mum has a shell from my grandad. It's next to her bed. You can hear the sea in it."

"That's it, Ellie my dear. Humans are feeling creatures, aren't we? What we touch, taste, hear, see, even what we smell..." She held up a flower. "It all helps us stay connected to the things we remember... what we love."

A sudden breeze blew a gust of blossom towards them. Ellie watched it fall.

"My nana loved her garden," she said, "but then she fell..."

Just then, Alan straightened up with a grunt and called over to them, "Awful lot of planting to do here, Laidee."

"Don't worry, Alan!" said Laidee, but Ellie could see he was right. Heaps of pots were stacked up untidily all around.

"Ellie is Maggie's granddaughter, Alan," Laidee went on. "You'll have two expert gardeners here to help later on, I'm sure."

"But..." Ellie was confused. "Mum said Nana's in a wheelchair now... how can she...?"

"Oh, it's all wheelchair friendly round here, don't you worry," said Alan. He made a sweeping movement with his arm.

"Nice wide paths, see... no steps... and what d'you think these blimmin' things are for?" He tapped the tray he'd poured the soil into.

"Park yourself up 'ere and off you go, just the right height. Your nana's been out every day this week. How 'bout fetchin' her now, eh? It might rain later."

Ellie couldn't believe it. She looked quickly at Laidee who clapped her hands and nodded. "Good! That is good! Now you are excited! Pick a plant to bring to her and let us go to find your nana!"

4

Sunflower House

The garden entrance to the Care Home was surrounded with tall bright yellow flowers growing out of wellington boots.

"Welcome to Sunflower House!" said Laidee.

Ellie frowned, "Sunflower...?"

"We have four different houses here, each with bedrooms and a dining room. Downstairs are flowers – Sunflower and Lavender. Upstairs are trees – Willow and Beech."

"A bit like school houses," said Ellie. "Which one is Nana in?"

"She is in Lavender, but Ellie, you know, we may bump into her in Sunflower lounge," Laidee glanced at her watch. "Yes, the dancing might have started already..."

Dancing...? thought Ellie as Laidee led her into a large, open dining room where two ladies in blue tunics were setting the tables with cutlery and flowers. Two much older ladies sat side by side in huge green armchairs. One of the ladies was holding a baby doll and humming as she rocked it gently in her arms. The lady next to her was waving a slipper very slowly to and fro in time to the soft music.

Ellie stayed back a bit as Laidee walked over to the ladies, smiling. "Hallo, my dears," she said, crouching down beside one of the armchairs. "Look, Ellie."

Ellie came forward a few steps until she was standing next to Laidee. "Peggy is holding a very special doll, here. You see it's breathing? It even has a heartbeat!" Ellie looked, and Laidee was right, the little doll's tummy was moving up and down underneath the old lady's hand. "Very special, isn't she, Peggy?" said Laidee.

Peggy smiled and looked like she might say something but then she bent her head back to the doll. She patted it just as if it was a real baby and started to hum again. Laidee turned to the other lady, but her eyes had closed. The slipper had fallen onto her lap. Gently, Laidee took it and placed it on the floor. She gave the lady's hand a little squeeze and then pushed herself back up onto her feet, beckoning Ellie to move with her towards the door on the other side of the room.

Ellie's head was whirling with questions but she didn't know how to put any of them into words.

For a moment they walked down a corridor lined with yellow flower prints without saying anything.

Then Laidee said, "Ah! You hear that?"

Music, floating down the hall. Ellie noticed there were musical notes stuck onto the walls, too, dancing cheerily above the flowers and leading them towards an open doorway at the end of the hall.

As Ellie looked through into a light and airy room she saw a young woman with a long ponytail, tall boots and an autumn-coloured guitar perched on the arm of another of the enormous armchairs.

Around her, a group of the oldest people Ellie had ever seen sat clustered in a loose semi-circle. Some were holding little coloured tambourines or bells, like the ones from the music room at school.

A tiny old lady in purple slippers was doing a shuffling dance with a much younger lady in a blue flowery tunic who Ellie was starting to recognise.

"Does that lady work here?" she asked.

"Yes, Sam is a carer here. A very caring carer! Dancing is such a beautiful way to start the day, isn't it?"

Sam was holding the old lady gently under each elbow as they swayed gently from side to side. She gave Ellie a little smile and wave.

"Hallo, everyone! Hallo, Jess!" Laidee called to the guitar player, who waved without skipping a beat.

Ellie scanned all the faces. Many of the people in the room had their eyes closed, "resting their eyes" as Nana might say, though some looked like they were really asleep and one very old gentleman with his head leaning right back against the chair was definitely snoring.

"Nana's not here," she said.

"I am sorry, Ellie," Laidee looked at her kindly.

"Sunflower's Friday morning music sessions usually attract quite a crowd! We are very lucky to have Jess with us each week. But let us head over to Lavender now. That is where we will find your nana."

Leaving the happy, bouncing sound of the guitar and the tinkling of bells, they walked on, but Ellie found herself walking slower than before.

❖

"You seem worried, Ellie," said Laidee as they walked down yet another corridor. "Please do not worry. You will see your nana very soon."

"It's not that," said Ellie. "It's just, the lady with the doll back there... and the lady with the slipper.... they looked like Jack does when he's just woken up from a nap. And, in the music room... it looked fun, but... everyone had their eyes closed?"

"Ellie, you are good at noticing things, eh? You know, one of the ladies in that room is 98 years old! When you have lived so many years, sometimes night and day get a bit mixed up, eh?"

"But what about... Peggy and the other lady? Why does Peggy have a doll? How come you know them but they don't know you?"

Laidee looked carefully at Ellie for a moment and then seemed to decide something. "My dear," she said, "Peggy and Val have a special condition called dementia. Perhaps you've heard of it?"

Ellie had. "It makes you forget stuff. My friend Shreya's grandad forgets everything. He lives with her, and she said one time he went out and left the door open and he couldn't find the way back and her dad had to go and look for him."

"Dementia affects the brain in a lot of ways, Ellie. It can be confusing. It is hard for Val and Peggy to remember my name, sometimes even my face. They met me only when they moved in here. Sometimes they may seem to forget where they are. They may feel they are somewhere else, yes? Maybe, some*when* else... back in their past. That can be very confusing, yes, for everyone."

"Okay, but... what about the doll?"

"Peggy is happy when she is holding her doll. It looks strange to us. But for her, she may feel she is back in her house with her own little baby. That would be many years ago for us, but it may feel like now for her. That is her moment, back when her children were little. It is our job to meet the person in their moment, yes? We make sure they are happy and comfortable, whenever it is. Yes. Happy, comfortable and safe."

"Is that why the doors are locked?"

They had reached a door with a punch-pad to type in a code.

"Ellie!" Laidee exclaimed. "You *do* notice everything!" She pulled away from the door and bent down a little to look at Ellie's face. "Everyone here can move around freely, Ellie. But in Sunflower, yes, we take a little bit of extra care. Remember Shreya's grandad?"

But Ellie was thinking about something else.

"Shreya said sometimes her grandad forgets her. He thinks she's her mum."

"That must be very hard for Shreya..."

"Will that happen to Nana?" Ellie interrupted. "Would she forget me?"

"I can see you are worried. Your nana does not have dementia, Ellie. But you know, even if she did... even if she ever forgot you here," Laidee tapped the side of her head, "she would always remember you..." she placed a hand over her heart, "here. You must tell your friend, okay? Even when we forget facts, we do not forget feelings. Come, let us find your nana."

Ellie nodded. She wished Shreya was here. She had thought the Care Home would be like hospital, but so far, it hadn't been like hospital at all. It was confusing.

As she followed Laidee she tried to remember what Mum had said about why Nana had to come here. It was all a bit fuzzy now. Why *had* Nana come to live here?

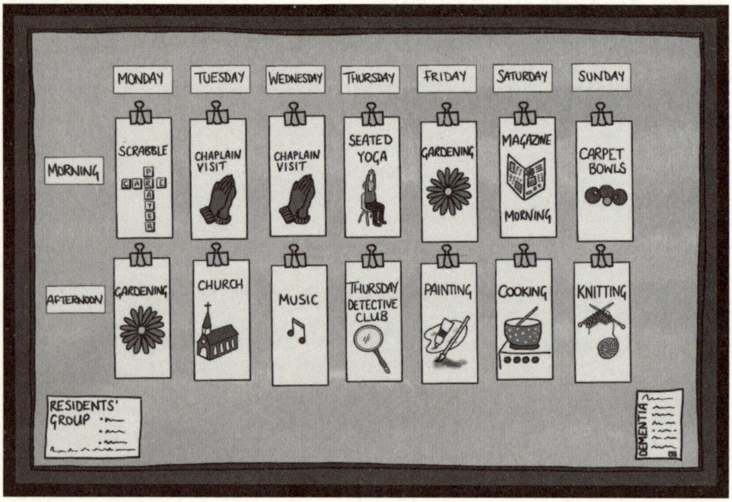

5

A Place Where People Live

They stepped through the door and Ellie was startled by a loud "ding!"

"Good morning, Rose!" called Laidee, and Ellie saw an old lady with snow white hair and a pearl necklace being wheeled out of a lift. A very small boy, who looked younger than Jack, sat in her lap.

The carer pushing the wheelchair stopped just in front of Ellie and Laidee and greeted them while the lady leaned forward and smelled the flowers in Ellie's pot.

"You know you can eat these, don't you?" Ellie wasn't sure if she was joking.

"Oh yes, lovely these are, in a salad. They for your granny or grandad, are they?" The old lady looked straight up at Ellie with very blue eyes.

“My granny. Er, I mean, my nana. We’re going to plant it in the garden.”

“Is that right? The work’s all finished out there, is it, Laidee?”

“Looking lovely,” said Laidee. “We just need to get a few more plants in the ground!”

“What about that, then, Charlie? You want a play outside? Dig in the mud?” and the little boy nodded eagerly.

“Kay,” said Laidee to the carer, “this is Ellie, Maggie Hodson’s granddaughter. We are just going into Lavender now.”

“Ooh, great!” Kay said. “I’ve heard a lot about you, Ellie. Your nana’s been looking forward to you getting here.”

“You’ve talked to my nana?” asked Ellie.

“Yes!” laughed Laidee. “Kay works on Lavender, Ellie, she is one of the people who makes sure your nana is well looked after.”

"Oh, Nana hates being looked after," said Ellie. It was out of her mouth before she could stop it. "I mean," she stammered, worried about seeming rude. "I mean, it's just she hates hospitals and things... well, she more likes looking after people really..."

Rose chuckled. "Atta girl!" she said. Laidee was smiling, and Kay too. She said, "It's alright, hun, I know what you mean. We try and make people feel at home, here, isn't that right, Rose? If people are independent, that's great."

Rose nodded and reached out to Ellie and her flowerpot. "You know these are called *Heartsease*, don't you?" She patted the flowers and then Ellie's cheek.

"You'll do your granny the world of good, coming here," she said firmly. "Ooof, Charlie! Sit still, there's a good boy, and there'll be ice cream later! See you again, Laidee. Push off to the garden, then, shall we, Kay?"

"Right you are, Rose," said the carer with a little salute. "Lovely to meet you, Ellie. See you later, Laidee."

Ellie watched them go, and Laidee put a hand on her shoulder.

"Rose is right, Ellie. Your nana will be so very glad to see you. But," she added, "I think you will be just as glad to find her too, yes? Come on, let us go."

❖

It wasn't quite time to meet Mum and Jack yet so Laidee led Ellie into Lavender House through the cafe. "It's like a real cafe!" said Ellie in surprise. The counter was piled high with cakes and biscuits and all the tables were full of families.

"This is where we have all our parties, too," said Laidee.

"Parties?"

"Yes, it is always someone's birthday! You know, we find a reason to have a party almost every week!"

Ellie didn't know what Nana would make of that. She never wanted to celebrate her birthday at home.

"I'm too old!" she always said.

Ellie looked around at all the families – she couldn't help noticing that there weren't that many kids her age.

Laidee guessed what she was thinking. "Come back on Sunday, Ellie! You will meet lots of children of all ages!" said Laidee. "I will introduce you."

As they left the cafe, Ellie noticed a table with a big framed black and white photograph of a very beautiful lady. There was a large candle burning in a glass jar in front of it, and white flowers surrounded the photo and covered the table. Someone with beautiful curly handwriting had written "~ *In Loving Memory* ~ *Elizabeth Morris* ~"

All of a sudden Ellie felt much too hot.

Chewing on her lip, she followed Laidee into a wide corridor lined with a row of doors, then stopped again in surprise. It was like being in an indoor street. The doors were real front doors, like you'd find on a house. Each was painted a different bright colour and had a number made of brass in the middle.

Next to each door was a little box with a glass front.

Curious in spite of herself, Ellie stood on tiptoe to peer into one.

Stuck onto the back of the box was an old football ticket, a black and white picture of a man and a lady outside a church, and a silver medal on a ribbon. A battered old tin that said "Leonard" in big black lettering sat neatly under a red and white scarf.

The next one along had white lace stuck all around it, an assortment of buttons, a squashy yellow ball with pins and needles stuck in it, an old postcard of a beach in Devon, and a picture made of dried flowers stuck on cloth, signed Ella.

EMPIRE STADIUM · WEMBLEY
Association Football
INTERNATIONAL MATCH
ENGLAND v WEST GERMANY
Wednesday, Feb. 23, 1966
KICK-OFF 7.45
7/6
H 21
STANDING
BRITISH PENS LIMITE
Leonar

Laidee stopped to wait while Ellie looked. "They are memory boxes," she said. "You find them in most care homes, I believe."

"To remember people who have died?"

"No, dahling!" exclaimed Laidee, sounding shocked. "The objects in the boxes are things people love, and love to talk about! It helps us get to know people, and helps them remember which room is theirs too. When you move away from your own home, it can be hard to find your way around at first."

"Oh," said Ellie. "Will my nana have one?"

"Maybe not yet, but yes, if she wants."

"When we got here, I thought there were flats inside for people to live in," said Ellie.

"Some homes are like that," said Laidee, "but we support people who need a bit more help day to day. Everyone here has a private room."

"Does that mean they're on their own?"

"It means, just for them, a private room that no-one else shares."

A bit of Ellie wanted to ask more about the private rooms. Were they, like, just bedrooms?

But instead she found herself blurting out something she'd been thinking about ever since Mum had told her about the Care Home.

"Is this a place where people come to die?"

"Oh Ellie, my dear," said Laidee, but she didn't look surprised.

❖

They sat down in a window seat that looked out onto a little courtyard.

"You have been worrying about this, haven't you? Let me tell you, Ellie. Truly, this is a place where people come to live!"

"Not a place where people come when they're dying, then?"

"You might be thinking of a Hospice, Ellie," said Laidee in a very kind voice. "That is a special place where people do go to die in peace. This is a Care Home, a caring place, and people come here to live. You know, many times, they are more independent here than they could be at home. You know what independent means?"

"They can do stuff by themselves."

"Right! And what they want to do, as much as possible."

"But everyone here is so... *old*. People must die here. I just saw... I mean, the picture on the table, with the candle?"

Laidee smiled. "Yes, Betty. She was 89 and she died last week. You are right, Ellie. People are old. And they do die here. But not before they have lived! I promise you, we do our very best to make sure people can live as fully as they can, right up until the end. That can be many years! When the end comes, we do everything we can to make sure it's a good end."

"What do you mean a good end?"

"Perhaps we should wait until we find your mother before we talk about this?"

"Mum won't talk about it. She can't even talk about Grandad, and he died before I was born."

"I see. It can be very painful for those who are left behind. You know, we believe that death is part of life, Ellie, so we try to make it easier to talk about. So... a good end? Well, perhaps someone wants to have some special music, or a prayer, or for someone special to be with them... we can help to make that happen. As much as we can, we try."

Ellie hugged her knees. She didn't know what to say.

"I can see you are still worried, Ellie. Please do not be worried. Just now, your grandmother is in good health and good spirits..."

"Then why does she have to come here?" Ellie cried.

She felt her cheeks going red. She hadn't meant it to come out that loud, but Laidee didn't seem to notice.

"This must be a question for your mother, and for your nana," she said. "Let us go – we must find them. Come, my dear," Laidee's smile was very warm. "Your mother and brother will be waiting."

Ellie uncurled herself from the window seat and fell into step with Laidee as they headed back to the cafe. She felt weirdly sleepy. More than anything else in the world right now, she wanted to be in Nana's house, with the radio on, and the flowers on the wall, and Nana coming in from the garden smelling of earth and tomatoes and wrapping her up in a big Nana-hug.

6

FINDING NANA

They found Mum and Jack at a table in the cafe covered with felt-tip pens and muffin crumbs.

Laidee stayed for a quick cup of tea to wait for Nana, but she hadn't arrived yet and Laidee had to get back to the sensory garden.

"Thank you so much for showing Ellie around," said Mum, attempting to brush up the crumbs with her hands.

"It was a pleasure!" beamed Laidee. "Please say hallo to Maggie for me."

"Of course. She'll be sorry to have missed you. I can't think where she is. She was supposed to be here 20 minutes ago," said Mum, looking at her watch.

Laidee turned to Ellie and said, "You will bring your nana down to the garden, yes? Before Alan loses patience and starts planting everything himself, eh?"

Ellie nodded.

"We are very glad to have your nana here, my dear. And I am always here to talk to, eh?" She held out her hand for Ellie to shake, just like an adult.

Ellie shook it. "Thanks Laidee, see you later." She wished Laidee didn't have to go.

With a cheery wave to Jack, Laidee bustled out.

"What if Nana's forgotten us?" Ellie said out loud.

"Don't be silly, Ellie! She's probably just fallen asleep in her room." Mum stood up. "Come on, let's go and find her."

Clutching his red felt-tip tighter, Jack put a chubby hand over his drawing.

"Come on, Jack, let's go and find Nana."

"Not want." Jack stuck his chin out and didn't stop colouring.

Mum looked like she was about to tug the paper out from under his pen when Ellie said, "Jack, do you know, there's a *huge* garden out the back? When we've found Nana we're going to go and plant stuff in a big tub full of mud!"

Jack looked up. "Mud?" he said.

"Yeah," said Ellie, "and there's a bike with flowers in. I bet you could sit on it and push the pedals."

Jack thought about this and then carefully put the lid back on his pen.

Sensing movement, Mum went to the counter to pay and Ellie helped Jack roll his picture and get it into his bag.

"Careful," said Jack.

Ellie was about to tell him that she *was* being careful, *silly*, but then she looked at his face and saw his problem. He was quite proud of his drawing and worried it would crease, but he knew he couldn't get it in the bag himself without creasing it. He had to let Ellie do it, but he couldn't control what was going to happen.

"Don't worry, little bro," said Ellie, "I'll be careful."

Maybe that's why he suddenly said quietly, "Jack not want find Nana."

"Why not, Jack?" But Ellie thought she kind of knew already.

"Not want."

"Come on, Jack, what's the matter?"

"Jack's toys."

"Huh?" said Ellie.

Then suddenly she did know.

"Do you mean will she still have that special toy box for you? Nana's under-the-stairs box?"

Jack's face lit up and he nodded.

"Ah! Well... everyone just has a room here, so I don't think she'll have stairs. But she might still have the box. Shall we go see?"

After a moment's pause, Jack nodded again.

So, when Mum came back they were ready to go, with Jack holding Ellie's hand and the little backpack on his back.

"Oh," said Mum. "Right. Okay, good. Well done, Ellie. Let's go."

❖

Mum led the way into Lavender House. There was some painting going on at one of the tables in the lounge and Jack wanted to join in.

"Maybe on the way out," said Mum.

Ellie looked down at her brother and gently squeezed his hand. "Come on, we're looking for Nana remember?"

Then they came to the corridor with all the front doors and Mum stopped outside a leaf-green door with a gold number 6.

"There's nothing in the memory box," whispered Ellie.

Mum knocked and they waited.

There was no answer.

"Hmm, where is she?" said Mum under her breath.

"What if..." said Ellie, "what if she's fallen over in there and..." Ellie looked at Jack and didn't finish the sentence.

Mum was fumbling in her handbag for something. "We need to get someone to open the door and –"

"Nana!" said Jack.

"Hello, you!" called a familiar voice from down the corridor.

It was Nana.

Jack and Ellie ran to her. She looked so different from when they'd seen her in hospital. This lady with the shiny, bouncy grey hair and pink cheeks was the Real Nana come back. There was only one thing different.

"How do you like my new wheels, Jack?" Nana laughed.

"Come on, Ellie, what are you waiting for? Give us a hug! Come here, that's it!" And Nana leaned up a bit out of her chair and reached up for Ellie, and Ellie leaned down a bit and breathed in Nana's perfume. It was the same perfume. Ellie pressed her cheek on Nana's neck then pulled away.

"These are for you, Nana." She put the flowerpot in Nana's lap.

"Where have you *been*, Mum? We were about to get worried here!" Mum sounded cross, but she wasn't really, thought Ellie.

"I looked for you everywhere this morning, Nana," Ellie said, as Jack examined the wheels and tried to get them to spin.

"Can't an old lady go to the hairdressers?" said Nana, patting her new curls.

"We tried to get her to do her nails too!" said the young lady behind the wheelchair, whose own nails were long and blue.

"Maybe next time," Nana said. "Thanks Michelle, I'm sure Ellie and Jack can get me to my front door from here."

"You're welcome, Maggie, any time. I've got a nice apricot shade that will look good on you. Next time, okay?"

Mum smiled and shook her head, "I'd forgotten there was a salon here," she said. "We thought you might have –"

"Well, I'm here now," said Nana, "and all's well. Let's go in, shall we?"

Ellie and Jack pushed the wheelchair to the door while Nana fished in her handbag for her key.

"Here we are, home," she said brightly.

It was easy to push the wheelchair in, but Ellie only just got through the door before she had to stop and stare.

There was a fireplace and a mantelpiece with a photograph of Nana and Grandad Bill, just like at Nana's house.

And just above it, stretching all the way up to the ceiling, was Nana's green wallpaper.

7

Memory Box

"Imagine keeping a spare roll of wallpaper in the attic for 30 years," said Nana. She twisted around to try and see Ellie's face. "Knew it would come in handy one day."

There were the pictures in their silver frames from the living room. There was Grandad's old writing desk and the rug from Nana's bedroom.

There, by the bed, were Jack and Ellie's hand-print paintings that Nana had kept on the fridge.

The room was light and warm and the window had a cushioned seat so that you could sit and look out. Lavender stems were growing right up against the glass.

And under the window seat was a small wicker hamper, like a large picnic basket.

"Jack's toys!" shouted Jack, running straight to it.

"That's right, couldn't forget those, could I, Jack? What do you think, Ellie? Done a good job, haven't they?"

"It... it smells like your house, Nana," said Ellie.

Nana laughed. "That's 'cos I'm in it! Ooh, I've missed you – come and give me another hug. And let's find a place for those flowers."

"Actually, Nana, they're for the sensory garden here. Laidee, I mean Olaide, you know, the Chaplain – she gave me a tour. She thought we could plant it outside together."

Nana paused, holding onto Ellie's hand. Ellie couldn't help noticing how thin her skin was now – like crepe paper almost. "That's very kind of her," said Nana after a moment. "We'll do that then. I just need a quick cuppa first."

"Oh no, I forgot the kettle!" said Mum, hitting her forehead. "Sorry, Mum, I knew there was something. I'll go to the cafe and get us one."

"Not to worry, love," said Nana.

But Mum had already scooped up Jack and a handful of toy cars and swept out the door.

Nana raised her eyebrows at Ellie. "Needs a coffee, does she?" They both laughed.

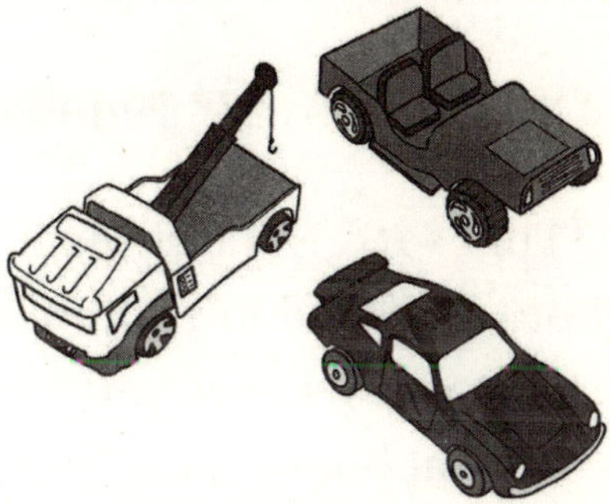

❖

Without Mum's bustling and Jack's zooming, it was quiet and peaceful in Nana's room.

"Now then, Ellie," said Nana, "will you help me with something?"

She leaned over and reached for a box on top of the dressing table with the mirror that had once stood in her bedroom. Struggling slightly, she pulled an old shoebox onto her lap. Ellie remembered it had once lived in the dining room dresser and was full of photos and cards and what Nana called her treasures. She sat down on the bed next to Nana's chair.

"Thought I'd save this to do with you. They have these little boxes outside all the rooms, Ellie –"

"Memory boxes!" said Ellie.

"That's it," Nana smiled, "well, as you know all about it, why don't you help me go through these and choose what to put in it, eh? Just like one of your scrapbooks. An Ellie Special."

Scrapbooking was Ellie's favourite type of project. She loved looking at photos, especially old ones.

"Who's this?" she asked, pulling one from the box. "I've never seen it before."

"That's your Mum and Uncle Richard on the beach, when they were little. Yes, that's a good one."

"What about this one of Oscar?" said Ellie.

"I think I'd rather have one of you and Jack, although that's a good one of him, isn't it, the hairy beast."

"Nana," Ellie exclaimed, "here's your house! Is that you and Grandad Bill? Why are you standing outside the front door like that?"

"Oh!" said Nana. "I'd forgotten I had that one." There was a pause. "That's the day we moved in."

"But, but..." said Ellie, "it's in black and white!"

"That's because it's old! Like me!" Nana did an odd little laugh and looked out of the window. "I lived in that house for 52 years..." Then, quietly, she said, "That house was my memory box, really."

"What's going to happen to it, Nana?" Ellie asked. She picked up a broken silver watch and pretended to try it around her wrist.

Nana started shuffling through the pile of photographs and postcards.

"I think I'll need to sell it," she said. Ellie looked up and saw that Nana's eyes were wet, but before she could think of anything to say, Nana said, "Now don't you worry about your nana, Ellie. I'll be alright."

"But why do you have to move here, Nana?"

"I need a bit more help to get around now, Ellie. Too many falls. Doctors think it's best. Your mum – well, better here than hospital. It's for the best, sweetheart."

"Will you like living here?"

"Yes, 'course I will. All the oldies, together, eh? And you visiting – that's all I need."

"Mum said Oscar can come and live here with you."

"Well, let's have a talk about that. Maybe he's gotten used to the end of your cosy bed by now."

"Can I stay over sometimes too?"

Nana hesitated. "Hmm, I don't know, Ellie. Don't know if that's allowed. Let's ask, shall we?"

Ellie looked up at the wallpaper.

"I wish you didn't have to move here, Nana," she said.

Nana leaned towards her over the empty shoebox and squeezed her hand so tight Ellie could feel wedding rings on her own fingers.

"I know, flower. Believe me, I do know."

All at once, all the crying Ellie had been holding in since Mum had told her about the Care Home flooded out in a salty, snotty mess. She tried to stop but she couldn't.

"Oh, now," said Nana, "there, there, it's alright. We'll be alright."

But to Ellie's horror, Nana was crying too. She was trying to hide it with her other hand, but Ellie could see the tears streaming through the powder on her cheeks.

Ellie quickly dragged her sleeve across her face and flung both arms around Nana. Before, whenever Ellie was upset, Nana would stroke her hair. Now Ellie was stroking Nana's hair, still bouncy from the curlers. She didn't know what else to do. After a minute that felt like forever, Nana heaved a deep sigh and laughed a raggedy sort of laugh.

"Oh, my dear! What a pair we are! What would Grandad make of me now, eh?" She tugged a tissue from her sleeve and dabbed her eyes.

"I'm sorry, Nana. I didn't mean..."

Nana waved a hand and cut her off. "You've got nothing to be sorry for. Let me tell you the truth, Ellie. I wish I didn't have to move here too." She held Ellie's hand tight. "But I'm alright. Really I am.

I'd much rather live here if it means I can be here with you and Jack and your mum. You're my real treasures."

Nana put her arm around Ellie and Ellie leaned her head on Nana's shoulder.

"And perhaps it's time I got used to a bit of being looked after myself, eh? At least in here I can still get about, do my own thing a bit."

"I love you millions, Nana," said Ellie.

"And I love you too, petal, millions and millions. And it's not far, is it? And soon you'll be getting the bus, and we'll have many, many happy afternoons here in the garden just like always, I can feel it. There now, Ellie, trust your old Nana."

Ellie blew her nose and wiped her eyes properly.

"That's my girl!" Nana gave her hand another squeeze.

"What about the memory box?"

"Let's leave it for now, eh? What's say we have our tea, then go and plant these violas you've brought me instead, and we'll finish the box next time. Let's make some new memories here first. How does that sound?"

"That sounds good, Nana!" said Ellie, and she threw her arms around her nana in another giant Ellie-hug.

SUMMER
Fair
PONY RIDES
* TOMBOLA
* PLANT SALE
* CAKE STALL
21/22 JULY
10 - 3PM
MHA

8

Heartsease

Just as they were putting the lid on the shoebox, there was a bump on the door and Jack almost fell into the room. He was holding a toy car in one hand and a carton of apple juice in the other.

Nana chuckled. "Watch out, littl'un!" she said.

Then Mum appeared with two cups of tea on a small tray and another carton tucked under her arm.

"Did you know there's going to be a summer fair here next weekend? With a pony, Ellie!"

"A pony?"

"Yes, I just saw the poster for it. We can't miss that. Maybe it's a little Shetland – that might just about fit through the gate." Mum laughed.

"But the garden's not ready," said Nana with a frown.

"Oh, Nana, I forgot to tell you," said Ellie. "Laidee says please come and help. There's loads of flowers everywhere in pots. We've got to get there before Alan plants them all himself."

"Plants them himself, is it?" said Nana. "Well, we can't have that, can we? Ellie, fetch me my gardening gloves out of that drawer there, will you?"

Ellie fished out the gloves and then, when Mum and Nana had finished their drinks, Nana said, "Right! Jack, where's your scooter? How about a race to the garden?"

Mum had left the scooter in the car, so Ellie pushed Nana's wheelchair while Jack ran alongside laughing. Nana joked she was like the queen, waving at people they passed. Her new neighbours, she said.

The garden was full of people and chatter when they got there. Rose and Kay were there, and the lady with the guitar, and Laidee was standing by the small table, laughing as always.

She came straight over when she saw them, arms wide and trowel in hand.

"Thank goodness you are here!"

Nana smiled and took the trowel from her. "Thank you for showing Ellie round the place, Olaide. Hear you need a bit of help with the planting?"

"It was a pleasure, and yes, please! Alan says we must have them all in by the end of the weekend!"

"Where are those flowers of ours, Ellie?" called Nana. "Let's start with those."

"Here they are," said Ellie and she held out the pot, remembering what Rose had called them. "Nana, a lady I met here told me we could eat these."

"She's right!" said Nana. And taking a petal, she ate it.

It was only a little joke, but Ellie laughed so much she felt dizzy.

They put the Heartsease flowers into the tub and Ellie watched as Nana set to work on the rest of the pots. It was even easier here than in her old garden.

Mum had been right. Nana was right. She was going to be alright. Maybe even more than alright.

A thought struck her. *And maybe there is a way I can do my homework.*

Ellie looked round the garden. At Laidee and her shells, Alan and his pots, and the swaying blossom trees. Mum was chatting to the carers and Jack was tumbling on the grass with Charlie, Rose's little grandson, while some other old ladies cooed over them.

She missed Nana's house, that was true, but maybe her Special Place wasn't Nana's House, after all. It was with her nana, so it could be wherever Nana's home was.

And maybe not everything was perfect, but it could still be special. They could still have many happy afternoons in this garden, just like Nana said.

And you know what?

They did.

My Special

Place

by
Eleanor
Hodson

Hi! My name is Eleanor Hodson and my most special place is with my Nana wherever she lives.

This used to be her house

This is her and my Grandad Bill standing outside on the day they moved in. It's black and white because photos were only black and white then.

This summer my Nana moved to a care home.

This is Olaide who I met when I first visited Nana at her new home.

What's A Care Home?

A carehome is a place where old people can live and be happier, instead of living on their own in a house with too many steps. Even if they do still love their house the carehome is safer and more fun.

Everyone has a room with a front door and a memory box so they have stuff to talk about and can find their way around.

There is a bigger garden and lots of flowers and people whose whole job is caring and helping.

(I would like to be a carer one day and an author and an photographer.)

↑ Surprise Birthday tea for Nana

My Nana lives on Lavender →

Everyone can have their own private room that they can decorate and make it look exactly like their old house if they want with lots of of their old stuff from their old house.

Even wallpaper!

The care home is a special place because it gives people freedom back a bit, and people care.

My Nana can still do gardening there and me and mum don't have to worry about her falling over.

Also I can visit whenever I like.

These are the flowers I planted at the care home with my Nana the first time I went there.

You can eat them, and they make your heart feel better.

I've left some scrapbook pages for you to fill in …

♡Ellie
x

Questions about care homes

What do you want in your memory box?

After Reading Follow-up

Thank you for reading *Finding Nana* – we really hope that you enjoyed it.

Sometimes stories can make us think of things that we want to ask more or talk about.

Here are some questions to help that you could share with a trusted adult.

- What do you think Ellie was feeling at the end of the story?
- How did the story make you feel?
- What questions do you have about when someone starts living in a care home?
- Ellie was feeling nervous about going to visit her Nana in the Care Home. Do you think you would feel the same way?
- If you have already visited someone you love in a care home, how did you feel about it?

To find out more about residential care homes and chaplaincy, you can visit the MHA website **mha.org.uk**

If you want to find out more about dementia, you can watch the *Memories with Grandma* video made by Dementia Friends at **dementiafriends.org.uk**

Ask a trusted adult to help you find these websites.

Meet the Author

Jenni makes a living by writing things down, finding things out and solving problems to help organisations do good in the world. She volunteers in schools and with Scouts and she's learning how to be a forest school teacher too.

Whatever else she's doing, Jenni is always a full-time wife, mum, daughter, sister & friend. She tries to be a good listener.

She wrote this book in memory of her Nanny & Grandad by listening as much as she could to the thoughts and feelings of those who live and work in MHA care homes.

Meet the Illustrator

Sophie is an artist based in Staffordshire. She can usually be found wearing wellies & in the company of a collie.

With a background in botany, much of her work involves plants - either as subjects for illustrations or planting design, or collaborating with them to create living sculpture, or installations.

Sophie says thanks to her daughter for Ellie's scrapbook handwriting, & to Jean Parmenter (Nanny P) for her inspiration. Sophie hopes she has the same energy when she's 95!

ABOUT MHA

Methodist Homes (MHA) is the largest charity care provider for older people in the UK, providing care for over 80 years. Our services include care homes, retirement living and community groups. It's our vision to inspire the best care and enable people to live later life well.

Inspired by Walter Hall, the Methodist Church in 1943 wanted to improve the quality of life of older people in the time before the creation of the Welfare State. Today, MHA continues to provide care to people of all faiths and none, providing accommodation and support to more than 18,500 older people across the UK.

As one of the very few charitable care providers in the UK, we are dedicated to reinvesting any surplus that we may receive back into the services we provide, including our specialist dementia care, chaplaincy support and music therapy.

We put people at the heart of everything we do, treating people as individuals, respecting, and honouring their wishes and providing care in a way that's best suited to each person's specific needs, enabling them to live later life well.

facebook.com/MethodistHomes
instagram.com/MHACharity
twitter.com/yourMHA

mha
Live later life well

About the Methodist Church

The Methodist movement was founded by John Wesley (1703-91). John Wesley believed, without question, that God's love is for everyone.

Today, the Methodist Church is one of the largest Christian churches serving Great Britain.

The calling of the Methodist Church is to respond to the gospel of God's love in Christ. We do this by getting to know and to serve our neighbours, living out our faith Monday to Sunday. We think that belief should lead to action that challenges unjust systems and brings positive changes to the world. You will find Methodists campaigning for climate justice, setting up advice centres and running food banks, warm spaces, schools and care homes.

The Methodist Church believes that all people are uniquely made in the image of God. It is committed to becoming a church that prioritises justice and dignity for all, where all are welcome.

If you would like to learn more about how the Methodist Church can welcome you, find your local Methodist Church at **methodist.org.uk/findachurch**.

Or follow us:
facebook.com/MethodistGB
instagram.com/methodistchurch
twitter.com/MethodistGB

The **Methodist** Church